Rising Stars

DEMI LOVATO

By Kristen Rajczak

Gareth Stevens
Publishing

RIGHT ON!

Please visit our website, www.garethstevens.com. For a free color catalog of all our high-quality books, call toll free 1-800-542-2595 or fax 1-877-542-2596.

Rajczak, Kristen.
 Demi Lovato / Kristen Rajczak.
   p. cm. — (Rising stars)
 Includes index.
 ISBN 978-1-4339-5888-5 (pbk.)
 ISBN 978-1-4339-5889-2 (6-pack)
 ISBN 978-1-4339-5886-1 (library binding)
 1. Lovato, Demi, 1992—Juvenile literature. 2. Actors—United States—Biography—Juvenile literature. 3. Singers—United States—Biography—Juvenile literature. I. Title.
 PN2287.L656R35 2011
 791.4302'80922—dc22
 [B]

                              2010046423

First Edition

Published in 2012 by
Gareth Stevens Publishing
111 East 14th Street, Suite 349
New York, NY 10003

Copyright © 2012 Gareth Stevens Publishing

Designer: Katelyn E. Reynolds
Editor: Kristen Rajczak

Photo credits: Cover, pp. 1–32 (background) Shutterstock.com; cover, p. 1 Frazer Harrison/Getty Images for PCA; p. 5 Gary Miller/FilmMagic; p. 7 Valerie Macon/Getty Images; p. 9 Arnaldo Magnani/Getty Images; p. 11 Mark Davis/Getty Images; pp. 13, 17 Frederick M. Brown/Getty Images; p. 15 Gareth Cattermole/Getty Images; p. 19 Jemal Countess/Getty Images; p. 21 Andrew H. Walker/Getty Images; pp. 23, 29 Ethan Miller/Getty Images; p. 25 Bryan Bedder/Getty Images; p. 27 Frazer Harrison/Getty Images.

Printed in the United States of America

CPSIA compliance information: Batch #CS11GS: For further information contact Gareth Stevens, New York, New York at 1-800-542-2595.

Contents

Meet Demi

Demi Lovato is a singer and actor.

She has performed all over the world!

Demi's full name is Demetria Devonne Lovato. She was born on August 20, 1992. Demi and her family lived in Dallas, Texas, when she was a child.

Demi's sister Madison

Big Dreams

Demi's mom is Dianna De La Garza. She was a cheerleader for the Dallas Cowboys football team. She was also a country singer. Demi wanted to be like her.

Dianna De La Garza

TV Time

Demi started acting when she was a little girl. She was on the TV show *Barney & Friends*. She met her friend Selena Gomez at the audition.

Selena Gomez

11

Demi appeared in a Disney Channel TV show called *As the Bell Rings* in 2007. Each episode was only 5 minutes long. Her work at Disney helped make her a star!

Disney Star

In 2008, Demi starred as Mitchie Torres in Disney's TV movie, *Camp Rock*. She sang with the Jonas Brothers. Almost 9 million people watched!

Kevin Jonas

Joe Jonas

Nick Jonas

15

Demi and Selena Gomez were in the TV movie *Princess Protection Program* in 2009. Demi's TV show, *Sonny with a Chance*, also started that year. She won a Teen Choice Award for playing Sonny Munroe.

Camp Rock 2: The Final Jam came out in the summer of 2010. About 8 million people watched it! By then, Demi had become a well-known actor and singer.

Nick Jonas

Joe Jonas

Kevin Jonas

19

Making Music

While Demi was becoming a TV star, she was also playing music. She sings and plays guitar and piano.

Demi's first album came out in 2008. It was called *Don't Forget*. It reached number 2 on the Billboard 200.

In 2008, Demi opened for the Jonas Brothers on their Burnin' Up Tour. She performed on her own and with the band.

Joe Jonas

Here We Go Again, Demi's second album, came out in 2009. It was number 1 on the charts!

Demi traveled the world in 2010. First, she went on her own tour in South America. Then, she was a special guest on the Jonas Brothers World Tour!

Timeline

1992   Demi Lovato is born on August 20.

2007   Demi stars in *As the Bell Rings*.

2008   Demi puts out her first album.
Demi stars in *Camp Rock*.

2009   Demi wins a Teen Choice Award
for *Sonny with a Chance*.
Demi puts out her second album.

2010   Demi stars in *Camp Rock 2: The
Final Jam*.

Books

Edwards, Posy. *Demi Lovato: Me & You*. London, England: Orion, 2009.

Rutherford, Lucy. *Demi Lovato & Selena Gomez: The Complete Unofficial Guide of the BFFs*. Toronto, ON, Canada: ECW Press, 2009.

Websites

Demi Lovato's Official Website

demilovato.com

Find out if Demi Lovato is appearing in a city near you.

Sonny with a Chance

tv.disney.go.com/disneychannel/sonnywithachance/

Read more about the characters of *Sonny with a Chance* and play games.

Publisher's note to educators and parents: Our editors have carefully reviewed these websites to ensure that they are suitable for students. Many websites change frequently, however, and we cannot guarantee that a site's future contents will continue to meet our high standards of quality and educational value. Be advised that students should be closely supervised whenever they access the Internet.

Glossary

audition: a tryout

award: a prize given for winning

episode: one part of a TV show's story

perform: to do something in front of a group of people

tour: when a person or group of people travels to different cities to perform

Index